JUNIOR MARTIAL ARTS
Safety

Junior Martial Arts

ALL AROUND GOOD HABITS
CONFIDENCE
CONCENTRATION
HAND-EYE COORDINATION
HANDLING PEER PRESSURE
SAFETY
SELF-DEFENSE
SELF-DISCIPLINE
SELF-ESTEEM

JUNIOR MARTIAL ARTS

Safety

SARA JAMES

MASON CREST

Mason Crest
450 Parkway Drive, Suite D
Broomall, PA 19008
www.masoncrest.com

Printed and bound in the United States of America.

First printing
9 8 7 6 5 4 3 2 1

Series ISBN: 978-1-4222-2731-2
ISBN: 978-1-4222-2737-4
ebook ISBN: 978-1-4222-9070-5

The Library of Congress has cataloged the
        hardcopy format(s) as follows:

        Library of Congress Cataloging-in-Publication Data

James, Sara.
  Safety / Sara James.
      pages cm. – (Junior martial arts)
    ISBN 978-1-4222-2737-4 (hardcover) – ISBN 978-1-4222-2731-2 (series) – ISBN 978-1-4222-9070-5 (ebook)
  1. Martial arts–Juvenile literature. 2. Safety education–Juvenile literature. I. Title.
  GV1101.35.J36 2014
  796.8–dc23
                            2013004759

Publisher's notes:
The websites mentioned in this book were active at the time of publication. The publisher is not responsible for websites that have changed their addresses or discontinued operation since the date of publication. The publisher will review and update the website addresses each time the book is reprinted.

Contents

MORE THAN FIGHTING

Karate. Taekwondo. Judo. Kung fu. What do all of these things have in common? They're all martial arts!

You might think that martial arts are all about fighting. Martial artists can take care of themselves in a fight. They can kick and punch. They can knock people to the ground. They can beat people twice their size.

All of that is true. But there's so much more to martial arts. When you practice martial arts, you learn how to defend yourself. But you also learn lots of other things. You learn how to be a better person.

Fencing students practice fighting each other with special swords. The swords aren't sharp and have a ball on the end. Students also wear pads and helmets to make sure they don't get hurt.

You learn how to feel good about yourself. You learn how to focus and concentrate. You get better at balancing. You get stronger. Martial arts help you do a lot of things better.

What Are Martial Arts?

There are a lot of different kinds of martial arts in the world. The very first martial arts were created thousands of years ago. All martial arts teach **self-defense.**

Today, martial arts aren't about fighting people or hurting others. Now people don't learn martial arts so they know how to fight. They learn them to get exercise. Or to become better people. Not many martial arts students use their skills in real-life fights. Martial arts are about much more than fighting.

Martial arts come from all over the world. There are hundreds of different kinds. Many of them are from Asia. Karate, aikido, and jiu-jitsu come from Japan. Kung fu (also called wushu) is a group of different kinds of martial arts from China. Taekwondo comes from Korea.

SAFETY

Martial arts come from other parts of the world too. Capoeira and Brazilian jiu-jitsu come from Brazil in South America.

There are also many martial arts from Europe. You might not think of them as martial arts, but they are ways of defending yourself. Fencing, boxing, and wrestling are all European martial arts.

Today, you can find each kind of martial art all over the world. You don't have to be in Japan to learn aikido. You can often find classes for different kinds of martial arts no matter where you live.

Every martial art is a little different. You have to learn different moves for each one. Some are done mostly standing up. Some are **practiced** on the ground. Some use weapons. Some are done with a partner, and some without a partner.

The people who teach martial arts are called masters or senseis. They have spent a long time learning their martial art. They teach all kinds of students, some very young, some very old. Martial arts can be learned as child or an adult.

In a martial arts school, students learn all sorts of things. They start out with basic moves, like how to stand. Then they move on to harder and harder things.

Students also learn other things besides moves. The teacher might have a lesson on how to stand up to bullies. Or how to feel good about yourself. You learn a lot of different things in martial arts class!

AIKIDO

Aikido is a martial art from Japan. A man named Morihei Ueshiba invented aikido. It was invented almost 100 years ago. Two people practice aikido together. One is the attacker. He runs at his partner. The other person is getting attacked. She learns how to throw the attacker to the ground. She uses his movement to throw him, instead of using a lot of strength. Safety is very important in aikido. The attacker has to know exactly how to move so that he doesn't get hurt or hurt his partner. The person being attacked has to know how to move so that she doesn't hurt her partner.

More Than Fighting   9

The skills you learn in martial arts can be a big help in school. You learn to listen, show respect, get along with others, and more. Martial arts is great for your body and your mind!

Beyond the Martial Arts Class

After you take martial arts classes for a while, you'll get better. You'll be able to do new things you couldn't do before.

Martial arts can help you outside of class too. They can make school easier. They can make your friendships better. It can make it easier to get along with your family.

How does all that happen? It has to do with all the extra things you learn from martial arts. Martial arts teach you many **skills** that have nothing to do with punches or kicks.

For example, let's say you learn how to respect people more through martial arts classes. Respecting people means thinking about their feelings and treating them well. Your martial arts teacher thinks respect is really important. She talks

SAFETY

about it a lot. You've learned to respect her. You respect your classmates. And you respect yourself.

You do better at martial arts because you know how to respect everyone in class. But learning respect also helps outside of class.

You respect your teacher at school. That means always paying attention to him. You follow the rules. You don't talk in class.

You'll probably do a lot better in school. Because you're paying attention, you learn more and do better on tests. Your teacher notices you being more respectful.

Your friends notice you're respecting them more too. You listen to what they say. You're nice to them. You don't make fun of them or yell at them. Because you respect your friends, they treat you better too!

At home, you respect your family. That means you follow the rules at home. You don't fight as much with your brothers and sisters. You don't get into trouble at home as much and you get along better with your whole family.

Martial arts can teach you a lot about being kind to others and feeling good about yourself. Karate and taekwondo are about a lot more than punches and kicks.

Safety

Martial arts are all about being safe. They teach you how to be safe if someone tries to hurt you. But martial arts can be dangerous too. You can get hurt if you don't know what you're doing. That's why you have to learn about martial arts safety.

Safety in martial arts means a lot of things. It means you're wearing the right clothes. It means you're practicing in the right place. It means you're not doing things that will hurt your body.

Before you start martial arts, you might not know all the safety rules. But if you're learning from a good teacher, she'll teach you about safety.

Safety is one of the first things you'll learn in martial arts. You can't learn how to do things until you learn how to be safe doing them. If you tried to throw someone to the ground, you could hurt yourself. Or you could hurt the person you're throwing. You have to learn how to be safe doing it first. Then everyone can have fun and not get hurt.

2

SAFETY AND MARTIAL ARTS

There are lots of things to think about when it comes to safety in martial arts. The point of safety is to not get hurt. There are important rules for martial arts students to follow to keep everyone safe and having fun.

Listen to the Teacher

Your teacher will tell you lots of safety tips. He'll also tell the rules you need to follow to stay safe.

Martial arts teach you how to fight. But they teach you how to fight in a certain way. You can't just fight any way you want. Martial arts aren't about hurting other people. Martial arts students fight each other for practice, but they aren't

A mouth guard keeps your teeth safe when you're sparring in class. If you get hit in the mouth, a mouth guard will keep you from getting hurt.

trying to hurt each other. Practice fighting is called **sparring**. Your teacher will tell you what you need to do to keep everyone safe.

You won't be allowed to bite or scratch. You can't pull people's hair or pinch them. You can't try to hurt someone on purpose.

Your teacher will tell you how to do each move. Teachers know how to do each one so that it doesn't hurt you or your partner. They'll tell you how to fall right. They'll tell you how to stand and punch so that you don't hurt yourself or others.

Your teacher will show you how to warm up before starting. Stretching your muscles will keep you from getting **injured**. You'll also do better in practice if you stretch first.

14   SAFETY

Your teacher will also tell you to drink lots of water. You might not notice that you need water during class. But drinking lots of water keeps you from getting dizzy. It also keeps your muscles in shape.

If you have any questions about safety, you can always ask the teacher. She'll be able to answer any questions you have. And she'll keep you safe!

What You're Wearing

You'll probably have a uniform you need to wear to class. Most martial arts uniforms are made out of light material. They have pants and a long-sleeved top. Karate students wear a kind of uniform called a *gi*.

You shouldn't be wearing anything that could hurt anyone. Jewelry could hurt someone if it hit them in the wrong place. So could belt buckles or things in your pockets.

Sometimes you need to wear special things to protect yourself. You might have to wear a helmet. Students wear helmets when they might fall, or if someone is practicing throwing them to the ground.

You might wear arm or shin pads too. If someone is practicing kicking you, it's a good idea to protect yourself with pads.

When you're practicing punches, you might have to wear a **mouthguard**. It keeps your teeth from getting hit.

Calm Down

Try to leave your feelings at the door of your martial arts school. You're more likely to hurt someone if you're really mad, for example.

You never want to hurt someone on purpose. If you're mad, you might lose control of your feelings. You'll hit and kick harder. You might not even know that you're hurting someone.

If you need to calm down, take a rest. It's better to sit and calm down than to hurt someone by accident.

Remember that hurting others is not part of martial arts. Martial arts aren't about using what you learn from a master or sensei against others. Being safe and calm lets everyone learn and have fun.

Weapons

In some martial arts, you might get to train with weapons. You have to be careful to keep safety in mind.

You might have swords. Or short or long sticks. Or knives. Whatever weapon you have, you need to be careful.

First, you'll learn the moves without the weapons. You'll have to pretend you have them in your hands. Make sure to listen closely to what your teacher says.

When you actually get to hold the weapons, go slow. Don't try to do everything all at once. Remember what you learned and practice over and over again. You can get faster once you're used to holding the weapon.

KUNG FU WEAPONS

People who do kung fu can choose to learn how to fight with eighteen different weapons. They include the cudgel (a long stick), spears, axes, and swords. Students learn the basic moves of kung fu first. Then they add in weapons. Only martial artists who have been learning for a long time can use all eighteen weapons. They have to learn how to be safe with every single one.

Injuries

If you follow all the safety rules in your martial arts school, you can avoid getting hurt. Of course, we can never be 100 percent safe. You still might get a little hurt once in a while.

Martial artists often get bruises. If you fall down or get kicked a little too hard, you could bruise.

Bruises aren't a big deal. They can look ugly, but they're perfectly normal. If it really hurts, you can put ice on the bruised part of your body for a few minutes. The bruise should go away in a few days.

Martial artists sometime **sprain** their ankles or wrists or knees. That happens when they pull their joints too far in the wrong direction. Or they get strains, when they stretch their muscles too far.

16

Sprains and strains can happen if you trip. Or if you jump and land wrong. You could also get a sprain or strain by punching and kicking.

These sorts of injuries happen to many martial arts students. You'll have to rest for a little while. If you get hurt like this, you might even have to take a day or two off from martial arts class. But you'll get better fast.

There are also more serious injuries. You could hurt your head. Falling or hitting your head hard could lead to a **concussion**. Concussions are when your brain gets pushed against your skull. They can get in the way of your brain working right.

Someone who gets a concussion might have a headache. She might forget things.

Some concussions are serious. No matter what, someone with a concussion should go to the doctor right away. Concussions don't often happen in martial arts, but you should know what to do if you or someone in your class gets a concussion.

People usually get better from concussions pretty fast. It will take a few days or a couple weeks. They shouldn't practice martial arts until they're completely better.

BEGINNERS

When you're just starting out, martial arts can be especially hard. You want to do all those fancy kicks and punches. But you don't know how yet. You might want to push yourself too hard. You might want to try to do things you have no idea how to do. That's not a good idea. It can seem frustrating, but you have to wait until later. If you try harder things, you could hurt yourself. First, you have to learn the right way to do simpler things. You have to learn how to stand right. You have to learn how to focus. Your teacher will help you figure out how much you can do. And don't worry—you'll get to the fancy stuff later!

Safety and Martial Arts   17

3

IMPROVING YOUR SAFETY

Staying safe can be a lot of work. But it's important for you to know what to do if someone is trying to hurt you or you get hurt while playing sports.

You can practice being safe every day. You can practice being safe in martial arts classes. You can also practice being safe at school, at home, and on the street.

Dealing with Bullies

Sometimes kids have to deal with bullies. Bullies are people who are mean on purpose. They tease other people. They might even try to hurt them.

A lot of kids start taking martial arts classes because they're worried about bullies. Some people might think about using martial arts to fight against bullies. But trying to hurt someone else isn't what martial arts are about. It's not okay to try to hurt others, even if they aren't being nice to you.

There are ways to stay safe whenever you have to deal with a bully. Even if you don't know martial arts, you can protect yourself.

If someone starts being mean to you, stand or sit up straight. Look the bully in the eye if you can. You can ask or tell the person to stop. It might be scary, but if you show the bully that you're in charge, he might back down.

Get away as soon as you can. Go to the other side of the playground. Or do work in a different part of the classroom. If it gets really bad, go tell an adult. Teachers and other adults can do something about bullies.

Martial arts can give you the confidence you need to stand up to bullies. Martial arts students learn to not let mean things other people say hurt their feelings.

ANTI-BULLYING CLASSES

One martial arts teacher in Washington leads a class on how to deal with bullies. He knows what it's like to be bullied. He says, "To be honest, I was bullied as a kid and I know how it feels to be the last guy picked for football and get picked on." As a teacher, he decided to help kids who are picked on by bullies. In class, students talk about different kinds of bullies. They talk about online bullying. And they learn how to stand up to bullies and be more confident.

Sports

Lots of people play sports. You probably at least play sports in gym class at school. When you play sports, you might get hurt sometimes. You can keep from getting hurt if you follow some safety rules.

Make sure you're wearing the right uniform and gear for your sport. If it's football, wear pads and a helmet. In soccer, wear shin guards. Wearing that stuff

20 SAFETY

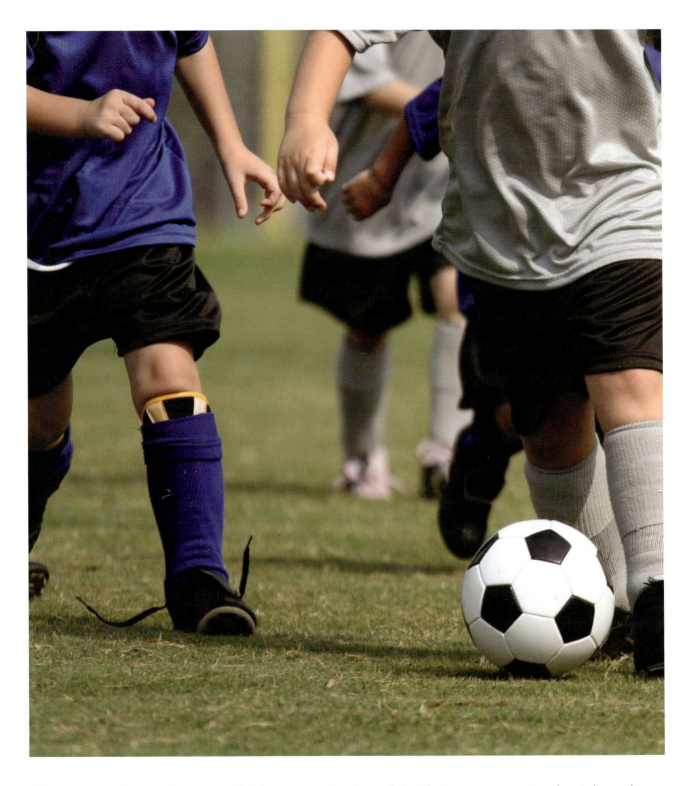

Whenever you're playing sports, it's important to play safely. That means wearing the right pads and clothes (in soccer, that means shorts and shin guards). It also means tying your shoes when running on the field.

might not seem like fun, but it will keep you safe. It's important to have the right **equipment** no matter what sport you're playing.

Like in martial arts, you should warm up before you start. Stretch your muscles. You'll feel better when you start playing.

It's best to first warm up by doing something easy like a few jumping jacks or walking around a little. Then you should do some stretches. You could touch your toes or hold your arms behind your head. Ask your coach or teacher what the best stretches are for you.

You should also drink lots of water and eat plenty of the right food. If you don't eat and drink, you could get dizzy. You won't be able to focus on playing your best.

If you get hurt, you'll have to rest. It can be hard to not practice with everyone else. You might even miss a few games. But it's better to rest. If you try to play with an injury, you could make it worse. Then you'll have to sit out even longer.

It's important to remember to drink lots of water when you're playing outside or practicing martial arts. Drinking plenty of water keeps you healthy and having fun!

Knowing the Rules

There are safety rules for many different things. There are safety rules when you're in a car, like always wear a seat belt.

There are safety rules for riding a bike—wear a helmet, always watch where you're going. There are safety rules for the kitchen, like don't use a knife unless an adult is with you.

Rules aren't made to be annoying. They're to keep you from getting hurt. Rules are there to keep everyone safe.

So always know the rules wherever you go. If you do something new, pay extra attention to the rules. Listen to the rules when you're playing a new sport, or flying on an airplane for the first time. Pay attention to the rules when you're cooking or traveling to a new place.

Knowing the rules can make new things less scary. If you're afraid to fly, for example, you might think you're not safe. But once you know all the ways you can stay safe while flying, you might feel better about it.

In Martial Arts

Keep your eyes open in martial arts class for ways you can be safe. You might see that there's a big gap in between two mats on the floor. Someone could step in the gap and trip. You should move the mats together. Or tell your teacher.

Always keep safety rules in mind. Don't walk across the middle of the room when people are practicing. You could get hit by accident. Or you could knock someone over.

Remember all the things your teacher has taught you. Warm up. Drink water. Wear a helmet or body pad. Try your best to do moves correctly. If you ever forget any of the rules, ask your teacher!

4

SAFETY AND YOUR LIFE

Safety helps make our lives better. You don't want to get hurt all the time. You want to feel good. You want to be able to do what you want.

You can use the safety rules you learn in martial arts outside of class. You can practice being safe using what you know from martial arts.

Safety is important in every part of our lives. Everyone should be safe at school, with friends, and at home.

Not Getting Hurt

A lot of the safety rules in martial arts have to do with not getting hurt. If we pay attention to safety, we don't have to worry about getting hurt as much.

In taekwondo, students wear padded helmets to keep from getting hurt. It's important to wear the right safety gear when sparring in martial arts class. That way, everyone can keep learning and having fun.

26 SAFETY

When you get hurt, everything is harder. You might have to miss school. You can't play your favorite sports. Maybe you can't play your instrument in the orchestra or band. You can't run around and have fun with friends.

Paying attention to safety means less time at the doctor's office. It means more time getting to run around and play. It means feeling good.

So keep your martial arts safety rules in mind outside of class. Remember that you should always wear safety gear when you do dangerous things. You should be careful when you handle things that can be dangerous (like martial arts weapons). You should take care of any injuries you have so that they don't get worse.

If you follow all the rules from your martial arts class, they'll help you be safe and happy in the rest of your life too!

TAEKWONDO SAFETY

There's a lot of kicking in taekwondo. You can get hurt if you don't know what you're doing. One way to not get hurt is to wear special safety gear. Taekwondo helmets are made to protect your head and neck. Sparring gloves protect your hands. Shin guards protect your legs. Some martial artists wear a chest protector too. Professional taekwondo martial artists know it's important to wear the right things!

Beyond Class

Your martial arts teacher might go over tips that have nothing to do with the moves you learn in martial arts. But they do have to do with staying safe!

You might learn to always be aware of what's around you. If you are looking all around you, you can spot danger before it happens.

Let's say you're walking home from school. Normally it's a safe thing to do. But today, there are some older kids walking toward you. They're laughing really loud in a mean kind of way. They look like they might be trouble.

Because you spotted them in time, you can cross to the other side of the street. Make sure no cars are coming, then cross over. The older kids stay on their side. Maybe nothing would have happened. But this way, you're sure to stay safe.

Your teacher will also probably talk about when it's safe to use martial arts outside of class. You probably won't ever have to use martial arts. But it's good to know when you can use them.

It's not okay to use martial arts anytime you want to fight. You should never start a fight. Martial arts are only for self-defense. You should only use martial arts if someone attacks you first. It's unsafe to use it any other time. Remember, martial arts are not about hurting someone else. They're about making your body and mind stronger. They're about safe fun.

You also shouldn't use martial arts on your brothers or sisters or friends. You can't use them just for fun. You could really hurt the other person.

Martial arts can help you outside class. Taking martial arts classes teaches you how to be safer. You can keep from getting hurt in and out of martial arts class just by following a few rules.

Martial arts can do lots of other things for you too. From teaching you how to respect people to helping you get stronger, martial arts do lots of good things. And all those good things will make you safer!

Words to Know:

concussion: A head injury caused by hitting your head that can leave you a bit con-fused for a little while.

equipment: The pads, balls, helmets, and other things you need to play a sport or join in an activity.

injured: Hurt or unable to play.

mouthguard: A piece of plastic that keeps your teeth safe when playing sports or practicing martial arts.

practiced: Learned, used, and trained to become better at something.

self-defense: Stopping another person from hurting you and making sure you're safe from danger.

skills: Things you learn that help you become a better person or live a better life.

sparring: Practice fighting.

sprain: Hurting a joint by pushing it too far.

29

Find Out More

ONLINE

The Black Belt Club
www.scholastic.com/blackbeltclub

Kid Safe Tips
www.kidsafetips.com

Kids Ask Sensei
www.asksensei.com/kids.html

KidzWorld: Martial Arts Quiz
www.kidzworld.com/quiz/5917-quiz-martial-arts-trivia

IN BOOKS

Iedwab, Claudio. *The Peaceful Way: A Children's Guide to the Traditions of the Martial Arts*. Rochester, Ver.: Destiny Books, 2001.

Peterson, Susan Lynn. *Legends of the Martial Arts Masters*. North Clarendon, Ver.: Tuttle Publishing, 2003.

Wiseman, Blaine. *Martial Arts*. New York: AV2 Books, 2010.

Index

About the Author

Sara James is a writer and blogger. She writes educational books for children on a variety of topics including health, history, and current events.

Photo Credits

www.Dreamstime.com
   Bowie15: p. 8
   Forsterforest: p. 22
   Joeygil: p. 18
   Johnkasawa: p. 26
   Keung1616: p. 10
   Neillockhart: p. 6
   Nickr: p. 12
   Rmarmion: p. 21
   Sai088: p. 14
   Withgod: p. 24